**W9-ABZ-103**

# Lions & Tigers

Konecky & Konecky
72 Ayers Point Rd.
Old Saybrook, CT 06475

English translation by Sean Konecky

© Losange, 2005
© Éditions Artémis for this edition
English translation © 2009 by Konecky & Konecky
10 digit ISBN: 1-56852-741-1
13 digit ISBN: 978-1-56852-741-3

Printed in India

# Lions & Tigers

Michel Cuisin & Pierre Darmangeat

KONECKY&KONECKY

# Contents: Lions

# Contents: Tigers

# Lions

➤ *Page 4 :* The lion is traditionally considered to be the bravest of all animals.

➤ *Page 10 :* The African lion remains plentiful only in national parks and other protected areas.

➤ *Pages 16-17 :* Looking at this lion with his magnificent mane, one can see why the lion is called the king of beasts.

➤ *Page 18 ::* Bengal tiger.

➤ *Page 18 :* This lion gives the impression less of being a formidable predator than a big lazy cat.

➤ *Page 19 :* With the lion, as with other felines, the front part of the head is low and wide, in contrast with what one observes in other carnivores.

➤ *Page 20 :* This picture of a lion's open mouth offers a good view of its long lower canine teeth. The lion's incisors are much smaller. There are three of them on each side of its lower jaw.

➤ *Page 21 :* As the lion ages his mane tends to become darker.

➤ *Pages 22–23 :* Not all lionesses and cubs climb trees. For reasons not known, the practice seems to be confined to certain localities.

➤ *Page 24 :* The lion's anatomy assures a particularly graceful and supple gait.

➤ *Page 25 :* The mane, characteristic of the male lion, is not found in any other species of cat.

➤ *Page 26 ::* Patty-cakes.

➤ *Pages 26–27 :* Lionesses are permanent members of prides.

➤ *Page 28 :* In this close-up of a lion's face, one can see the distinct grooves running from its eyes down each side of its muzzle.

➤ *Page 29 ::* Grant's zebras.

➤ *Pages 30–31 :* The lion's power is clearly evident as it drags its prey into the shelter of some shrubs to feed upon it away from scavenging hyenas. Lions have been known to bring down buffalos weighing up to 1,200 pounds.

➤ *Page 32:* Lioness stalking in high grass.

➤ *Page 32:* A spotted hyena *(Crocuta crocuta).*

➤ *Page 33:* Two lionesses attack a buffalo, whose front legs buckle under the weight of their assault. Buffalo will try to defend themselves with their horns but are not always successful.

➤ *Pages 34–35:* It has been observed that lionesses when hunting communicate with each other using strange muffled groans. Like the sounds made by a ventriloquist, it is very hard to pin down exactly where they are coming from.

➤ *Page 36:* A herd of buffalo.

➤ *Page 37:* This lioness takes a break after beginning her meal.

➤ *Page 37:* Once the lion's appetite has diminished, it tolerates the presence of cubs, who can then begin to feed. However, their allotment will depend upon the number of adults present.

➤ *Page 38:* Lions drink the blood of freshly killed prey, as well as ground water.

➤ *Pages 38–39:* Once they are sated, lions will go to sleep. The rest of their kill will be eaten by scavenging carnivores: hyenas, vultures, and marabou storks..

➤ *Page 40::* Lions' periods of activity are rather short: after a successful hunt, with a full stomach, they pass a good portion of the time digesting, resting, and sleeping.

➤ *Page 41:* The lioness pictured here will not venture to attack an elephant this size.

➤ *Page 42:* The members of a pride don't always stay as close together as seen here.

➤ *Pages 44–45:* In the heat of the day, lions will rest under shade trees or bushes. They are at their most active in the evening, night, and early morning.

➤ *Pages 46-47:* Compared to smaller felines, big cats walk with their bellies rather close to the ground.

➤ *Page 48:* The sparse whiskers of the lion have a tactile function; they are sensitive to vibrations, pressure, and contact.

➤ *Page 49:* The lion's mane is composed of some dark hair as well as some hair of the same shade as the rest of his coat. The fullness of the mane varies between individuals and regions.

➤ *Page 50:* Cats' tongues are raspy. They are covered with little bumps that help scrape meat from bones.

➤ *Page 51:* Portrait of a lion cub. Like adult lions, it has small ears and a big nose.

➤ *Page 52:* Remaining immobile, this lion blends into the background.

➤ *Page 53:* Like the domestic cat, of which it is often reminiscent, the lion likes to roll on the ground and sleeps with its belly in the air in a state of total relaxation.

➤ *Pages 54–55:* It looks like this lion cub is playing hide-and-seek.

➤ *Page 56:* Lionesses are the key members of their prides.

➤ *Page 56:* The fully grown male could easily swallow this young cub.

➤ *Page 57:* Through play, cubs exercise their muscles and gain self-assurance. Some games simulate hunting and capturing prey, clear evidence of an apprenticeship that will serve them later in life.

➤ *Page 57:* A young male lion whose mane is just beginning to come in. It will get darker as he grows older.

➤ *Page 58:* A lion cub is not always closely supervised by its mother. It may leave its hiding place when she goes out to hunt. Its coat remains spotted until it is about a year old.

➤ *Page 59:* Distancing themselves from the rest of the pride, the lion and lioness live together for a few days during which they couple frequently.

➤ *Page 59:* Distancing themselves from the rest of the pride, the lion and lioness live together for a few days during which they couple frequently.

➤ *Page 60:* A lioness suckling her cub.

➤ *Page 61:* Any lioness within a pride will take care of cubs. They do not have to be her own for her to suckle, groom, or watch over them.

➤ *Page 61 :* In the wild, lions' coats are often torn or damaged by thorny shrubs and other vegetation.

➤ *Page 62 :* This gives a clear picture of the lion's small incisors: six above and six below, neatly framed by its large canines.

➤ *Page 63 :* The head of the lion cub is not as round as that of an adult lion.

➤ *Page 63 :* In national parks with their tourists and rangers, lions become accustomed to the presence of people and their vehicles.

➤ *Page 64 :* Asiatic lion *(Panthera leo persica).*

➤ *Page 65 :* African lion

➤ *Page 66 :* It feels good to stretch.

➤ *Page 67 :* As a general rule, lions have better success hunting at night, especially if the moon is not bright.

# Introduction

All cats descend from a common ancestor that lived about 35 million years ago. They form a small group within the larger class of carnivores, and though they display wide differences in size and weight (from 3 to nearly 700 pounds), they share certain distinct characteristics. Cats have round heads, short snouts, and retractable claws. Their spinal column is extremely flexible, especially in the lumbar region, which allows them to make great leaps. Their soft wooly coats vary in color and can be striped or spotted. They all have strong jaws furnished with 28 or 30 teeth. When walking, they put their weight on the extremities of their paws and have a particularly elegant gait. Hearing and sight are the most developed of their senses. Most cats are solitary creatures (lions being an exception) and stalk their prey. Wild cats are present on every continent, except for Antarctica and Australia. They are not found in Madagascar, Japan, New Guinea, New Zealand, Sulawesi, or the neighboring islands.

# The King of Beasts?

According to popular notions the lion is considered to be the "king of animals." It owes this distinction in all likelihood to the adult males' luxuriant manes, which give them a regal look when in repose, but also to their earthshaking roars. Under the right conditions the lion's roar can be heard from as far as five miles away. One might also note that the lion is a somewhat lazy monarch. Adult lions spend four to five hours a day hunting or engaged in other activities. For the rest of the time they sleep or lie about in the shade.

Indeed, a case could be made that the African elephant is the true king of the jungle. Its size and behavior are more impressive. Others might bestow the honor upon the tiger. The Bengal tiger is often referred to as royalty. True, the tiger lacks the lion's mane, but it is a considerably larger animal. The great Siberian tigers of the Oussori River basin measure 10 feet from snout to tail and can weigh up to 800 pounds. The biggest lions are somewhat shorter and almost never exceed 550 pounds. Of course there are exceptions, as there always are in nature: in 1993 a male lion that was killed weighed 600 pounds and measuring over 10 feet in length, the largest specimen on record.

Nonetheless, the lion is credited with being the strongest and bravest of all animals. The Romans imported a large number for gladiatorial games. Under Pompey (106–48 BC) there were an estimated 600 captive lions in Rome, and according to Pliny the Elder (first century AD), there were on one occasion

Right:  *Looking at this lion with his magnificent mane, one can see why the lion is called the "king of beasts."*

more than 100 in the arena. The lion's high reputation has been transmitted in heraldry and the emblems and insignia of many lands, and persists to the present day. In the past, naturalists often spoke of it in unmistakably anthropomorphic terms. The late eighteenth-century French naturalist, Bernard Germain de Lacépède, described the lion in this way: "The lion's countenance is a mixture of nobility, confidence, seriousness and boldness. It shows forth the superiority of its limbs and the energy of its muscles." More prosaically, the lion is unique among felines: it is a social animal, living in groups in the wild.

Right: *Bengal tiger.*
Below: *This lion gives the impression less of being a formidable predator than a big lazy cat.*
Facing page: *With the lion, as with other felines, the front part of the head is low and wide, in contrast with what one observes in other carnivores.*

# The Lion's Place in the Animal Kingdom

The lion is a mammal, part of the order of carnivores and the family Felidae (felines), which comprises 37 species. It belongs to the genus *Panthera*, which consists of the big cats (in addition to the lion, the tiger, panther, jaguar and leopard). These are distinguished from other smaller felines—although cougars can be quite large—by certain anatomical characteristics and behaviors. Thus while eating, the big cats press their forelegs on the ground, while small cats hold theirs upright at an oblique angle. Big cats roar; small cats meow or purr. This characteristic is due to the structure of bones of the throat (the hyoids). The big cats have only one hyoid bone; instead of a second they have a small flexible ligament, which permits greater mobility in the larynx.

The zoological classification of the lion is somewhat fluid, since not all scientists in this field are in agreement. This has led to its being placed in the genus *Felis* by some and *Leo* by others. There are several subspecies of lion. Two have disappeared: the Atlas, Barbary, or Nubian lion (*Panthera leo leo*) and the Cape lion (*Panthera leo melanochaita*), whose habitat was the southernmost of all lions.

Facing page: *This picture of a lion's open mouth offers a good view of its long lower canine teeth. The lion's incisors are much smaller. There are three of them on each side of its lower jaw.*
Right: *As the lion ages his mane tends to become darker.*

# A Slow Decline

At the end of the Quaternary period, in the Pleistocene Epoch, cave lions (considered by some as a subspecies of today's lion) lived in Europe and Asia. Another subspecies, *Panthera leo atrox*, existed in North America. Finds show that the former lived in France. A skull was discovered in a cave in Vence (in the south of France) with a length of 14 inches, comparable to today's African lion, which ranges from 12 to 15 inches. These two subspecies disappeared during the last ice age. Apparently the lion ventured north from Africa during the period between two glacial eras. Other subspecies of lion are believed to have lived during the Pleistocene epoch: *Panthera leo fossilis* (early Pleistocene) and *Panthera leo spelaea* (middle Pleistocene).

The genetic links between the cave lion and the lion of today have recently been studied using DNA analysis on four bones discovered in southern Germany and three others found in Austria. The conclusion is that the cave lion was closer to today's lion than to any of the other big cats. It seems that the cave lion, isolated from its cousins in Africa and Asia, died out sometime during the Bronze Age, around the middle of the second millennium BC.

In classical antiquity lions inhabited southern Europe (in Greece, for example, from where they disappeared around 100 AD), in southern Macedonia, in Russia, and in the southeastern Caucasian region (from

Right: *Not all lionesses and cubs climb trees. For reasons not known, the practice seems to be confined to certain localities.*

Above: *The mane, characteristic of the male lion, is not found in any other species of cat.*
Facing page: *The lion's anatomy assures a particularly graceful and supple gait.*

where they disappeared in the tenth century). They were also found in Turkey, Lebanon, Iraq, Iran, southern Afghanistan, Pakistan, and north-central India. Lions existed in Syria until the nineteenth century. In 1860 lions still could be found in the Tigris and Euphrates river valleys. Once widespread in Iran, by 1870 they were confined to one area; the last was killed in 1930. Lions were living in northern India at the beginning of the twentieth century; the last lion in central Indian was hunted down in 1884. Today the only lions in India are found in the forest of Gir, northwest of Mumbai.

In Africa, the only continent on which lions are still widespread, their territories and numbers continue to shrink. At one time lions lived in Algeria and neighboring regions of the Tell Atlas and Aurès mountains. But they were already rare at the beginning of the nineteenth century, and the last one was killed in 1891. The same year saw the death of the last Tunisian lion; lions lived on in Morocco until the beginning of the twentieth century. Today lions inhabit only sub-Saharan Africa.

## Responsibility

The African lion remains abundant only in nature preserves and national parks, mainly in the south and east of the continent. Throughout Africa, outside of these protected areas, it is becoming increasingly rare, especially in West Africa, where its numbers have significantly diminished. Among the countries where it was most widespread, according to a 1995 survey, are Botswana, the Central African Republic, Ethiopia, Kenya, Zaire, Tanzania, and Zambia. The same survey reported that lions had practically disappeared from Mauritania, Lesotho, Togo, and Swaziland. The latest estimates put the number of lions remaining in the wild at somewhere between 16,500 and 47,000, with the population declining by 30 to 50 percent within the last two decades. Humans are primarily responsible for this decline. We have hunted lions for centuries and still do so, mainly where they pose a threat to livestock. In addition, just as for many other animal species, the relentless expansion of human population and the cultivation of former wilderness areas have reduced the lion's natural habitat. Certainly some African countries have outlawed lion hunts, and others have strictly limited them. But in other places the practice is still not illegal. Finally, in spite of all legislation, poaching continues, and lions that are considered dangerous to humans are killed.

The use of poison has also taken its toll on the lion population. In some places people try to eliminate various predators by poisoning animal corpses. Lions, who are scavengers, pay the price. The problem is particularly severe in those areas in which domestic animals are bred.

Right: *Lionesses are the permanent members of prides.*

Below: *Pattycake...*

# The Lion's Varied Diet

As with other felines, the lion possesses all the characteristics that make for a successful hunter: sharp eyesight and excellent hearing, a good sense of smell, retractable claws, which remain sharp since the lion walks on the pads of its feet, and powerful teeth (the canines, in particular). In addition, its last upper premolar and its first lower molar are sharply pointed, perfectly adapted for killing prey and tearing its flesh.

The lion's diet is varied, depending upon the types

of animal life in its locality and upon its sex. Male lions living within a pride hunt fairly infrequently. It is the lionesses, who are more numerous and more agile, who kill most of the prey. Solitary lions are often formerly dominant males who have been evicted from their pride by younger males. They may well be of an advanced age and bear wounds resulting from the struggle to oust them. Normally they content themselves with smaller prey and may attack livestock, even humans upon occasion. They have been known to eat termites, fish, and scavenge the corpses left by other predators. The preferred prey of healthy lionesses include Burchell's zebra, antelopes (Thomson's and Grant's gazelle, topi, hartebeest, and sometimes oryx), black-tailed gnu, as well as wild boar. On occasion lionesses will attack young buffalos, elephants, black rhinoceros, baboons, even young crocodiles, as well as certain birds.

A male lion can eat up to 80 pounds of meat at one sitting, a lioness as much as 50 pounds. But they don't eat like that every day. Lions can go a week between meals. On average an adult lion will kill about twenty large ungulates over the course of one year.

Left: *In this close-up of a lion's face, one can see the distinct grooves running from its eyes down each side of its muzzle.*

## Skillful hunters

Lionesses bear the primary responsibility for hunting for the prides of which they are members. They quietly approach large groups of prey occupied with grazing. Depending on the number of lionesses hunting together, the weaker ones will beat the grasses for prey, while the stronger and more aggressive individuals will launch the attack. They try to get as close as possible, rarely more distant than 20 to 50 yards. In general, lions will abandon their pursuit if they have not caught their victim after chasing them for 50 yards, though pursuits of 200 to 300 yards have been witnessed. If gazelles are the prey, several lions may hunt and kill one each; for larger game, two or more lions will attack together. A lion can reach a flat-out speed of 40 miles per hour, but this is considerably slower than that of an antelope. Thus they depend primarily upon the element of surprise. Close observations of the lion's hunting behaviors have been made by scientists who follow them in cars in national parks, where lions have grown accustomed to the presence of vehicles. Here are a few examples of their observations.

In the Serengeti National Park (Tanzania-Kenya), two lionesses, accompanied by four cubs, prepared an ambush for a group of zebras, which they had espied from about half a mile away. One lioness failed in her attempt, but the other succeeded, and they

Below: *Grant's zebras.*

Following spread: *The lion's power is clearly evident as it drags its prey into the shelter of some shrubs to feed upon it away from scavenging hyenas. Lions have been known to bring down buffalos weighing up to 1,200 pounds.*

both dined on the victim (the young having been left behind at a considerable distance). In 1969, also in the Serengeti, during the rainy season, the naturalist G. Schaller observed 121 meals. Half of these were on animals hunted down by lionesses, a quarter were the victims of hyenas. The inverse of this was sometimes the case as well. In one instance he saw two lions leaving a zebra they had killed to a band of 15 hyenas.

It can take a lion up to 10 minutes to dispatch its prey. It suffocates its victim by biting its snout. Or as has been observed in the Kalahari (Botswana-Namibia) and in other places, a lioness will leap onto an antelope's back, thus breaking its spine. Lions are strong enough to be able to kill cattle or other animals

Above: *Lioness stalking in high grass.*

Left: *Spotted hyena (Crocuta crocuta).*

Facing page: *Two lionesses attack a buffalo, whose front legs buckle under the weight of their assault. Buffalo will try to defend themselves with their horns but are not always successful.*

of similar size with a swipe of their claws. In South Africa lions hunt wild boar. Their chances for success increase if there are bushes or tall grass through which they can sneak up on an isolated victim. Male lions rarely hunt, in part because their distinctive manes make them too conspicuous. Hunting usually, but not always, takes place in the early morning or at night. In South Africa lions have often been seen hunting at waterholes where ungulates come to drink. The lion is always on the lookout.

## The struggle for survival

How do ungulates react to the lion's attack? In the Serengeti, the black-tailed gnu flee lions when they come within 40 to 60 yards, the Thomson's gazelle takes flight on perceiving a lion within 50 to 300 yards, but buffalo and giraffe will not run unless the lion comes considerably closer. As a general rule hippopotamus and rhinoceros adults ignore the presence of lions. If flight is not an option, some animals have the potential to fight off an attack. V. B. Dröscher, a German naturalist, reports that one of his guides saw a lioness let go of an oryx that it had captured. The oryx had thrust its long pointed horns into the flanks of a second lioness who had approached it. Four days later this lioness died of her wounds. In general, a lion who is visible does not pose a threat to antelopes, but astonishing reactions on the part of potentially vulnerable prey have been observed. In the Serengeti, Dröscher saw a lion watching a group of Thomson's gazelles at a distance of about 300 yards. To his

Left: *When hunting, lionesses communicate with each other using strange muffled groans. As with the sounds made by a ventriloquist, it is very hard to pin down exactly where they are coming from.*

great surprise, he saw the gazelles approach the lion en masse to within a hundred yards, all the while staring at it. Apparently disconcerted by their scrutiny, the lion retreated, but the gazelles followed after it for some miles before running off at high speed.

Even several lionesses together will avoid taking on a troop of buffalo, since they are dangerous adversaries. A group of lionesses may try to separate a mother giraffe from her young; the giraffe will often try to drive them off, kicking at their heads and sides, sometimes with success. But sometimes the lions will gain the upper hand and kill both mother and child. Lions will usually retreat from packs of wild dogs.

The behavior of lions is not fixed. As the pioneering naturalist George-Louis LeClerc du Buffon wrote, "In nature, nothing is impossible; expect that anything that can occur, will occur." Thus lions who normally act to beat game can also participate in the attack.

It sometimes happens that lions will steal prey from

Above: *A herd of buffalo.*

other predators. Four lions succeeded in driving off a pack of hyenas who had killed a zebra and were eating it on the spot. Finally it is not altogether rare for a lion to cannibalize one of its own that has been killed by another, and during the battle for dominance in a pride, the victor may sometimes feast upon the vanquished.

**A changing diet**
During the dry season, when the large herds of gnu and zebra leave the Serengeti and travel north in search of better pasturage, the lions do not generally follow them, contenting themselves with other ungulates who live in smaller groups, such as impalas or gazelles. Impalas, however, have learned to avoid the attacks of lions by frequenting places where there are an abundance of ticks and other parasitic insects.

Impalas delouse themselves, by reciprocal grooming and by cooperating with oxpeckers, which are a type of sparrow similar to a starling. These do not venture near to lions, but regularly clean the coats of large antelope, giraffe, and buffalo.

### The male's role

Once the lionesses have succeeded in the hunt, the males assert themselves, taking literally the lion's share. They become extremely aggressive, chasing the females and cubs away by roaring and swiping at them with their paws. Once they have eaten their fill, the lionesses can take their turn. The young are last in line; some of them will die of malnourishment.

Above: *This lioness takes a break after beginning her meal.*

Below: *Once the lion's appetite has diminished, it tolerates the presence of cubs, who can then begin to feed. However, their allotment will depend upon the number of adults present.*

# Predators and Parasites

The adult lion has no predators unless he is enfeebled by old age, sickness, or injury, although lion cubs on their own are at risk of being grabbed by hyenas or other big cats. Lions are, however, threatened by insects and spiders. The population of blood-feeding insects (who sting or bite in order to drink blood) can vary dramatically from locality to locality and from year to year. Near to Serengeti National Park is the extinct volcanic crater of Ngorongoro. It has a 10-mile diameter and is surrounded by low mountains. In it lives a small largely isolated population of lions (about 100 in all). Some years parasites are so numerous that they can weaken these great felines. In 1962 all except ten died; in 1963, a naturalist studying the area noted that he had seen only a few sexually mature lions and lionesses. In 1965 and 1967, the population reestablished itself. Several prides were founded by lionesses (six in 1972, when there were again about 100 lions of different ages). Sickness can also threaten lion populations; in the Serengeti Carré sickness killed more than one third of the population, about a thousand animals.

Below left and facing page: *Once they are sated, lions will go to sleep. The rest of their kill will be eaten by scavenging carnivores: hyenas, vultures, and marabou storks.*

Below right:*Lions drink the blood of freshly killed prey, as well as ground water.*

# The Lion's Role in African Ecology

The proportions of lion populations and their prey vary throughout East Africa. In Tanzania, it has been reported that there is one lion for 292 ungulates; in the Ngorongoro crater the proportion is one to 260; in Zaire's Albert Park, one to 360. (Elephants and rhinoceros are not included in these calculations.) According to a study done in the Kafue National Park in Zambia, lions hunt 19 species of ungulates, compared with leopards, who hunt 22 species.

The lion's role in the general ecology is similar to that of the other predators: hyenas, small cats, reptiles, large birds of prey. The lion limits the population of herbivores, thus ensuring their continuing health and survival. Its numbers, as those of other predators, are considerably less than those of its prey. An intensive study conducted in the Serengeti in 1967 found 3,000 lions, 3,000 hyenas, 360,000 gnus, 243,000 gazelles, and 280,000 zebras. Other predators live off the ungulates as well. The lion does not have a negative impact on the population of ungulates, since its prey is quickly replaced through reproduction.

In place where prey is less numerous (in the Kalahari, for example), the lion population diminishes. The population density lessens as well; the hunting range for a pride can reach up to a thousand square miles (in the Etosha National Park in Namibia). In contrast,

Facing page: *Lions' periods of activity are rather short: after a successful hunt, with a full stomach, they pass a good portion of the time digesting, resting, and sleeping.*

Below: *The lioness pictured here will not venture to attack an elephant this size.*

in Kenya, the highest population has been registered in the Masaï Mara Reserve, where there are 20 lions per square mile, with a pride's hunting range shrinking to 15 square miles. Given these figures and the lion's ability to adapt, only the intrusion of people or a foreign species can exterminate or severely threaten the survival of the species.

## An interconnected system

One can come to a better understanding of the lion's role in its environment by looking at only a fraction of the food chain of which it forms a part. There is no way of conveying its full complexity, but the schematic diagram on page 43 provides a model of savannah ecology. We have arbitrarily placed the lion at the center and use arrows to show the direct and indirect influences each species has on the others. The animal and vegetable species that support the prey of other animals are included as well. To depict the totality of interrelationships, the table design would quickly become unmanageable since it would need to include hundreds of thousands of species. But even this limited schema shows that the lion is but one element in a vast interdependent web of life. This tends toward but never truly achieves a state of equilibrium, which would mean that it had become static. Populations depend upon a number of varying factors.

Below: *The members of a pride don't always stay as close together as seen here.*

Following spread: *In the heat of the day, lions will rest under shade trees or bushes. They are at their most active in the evening, night, and early morning.*

# Feeding Relationships on the Savannah

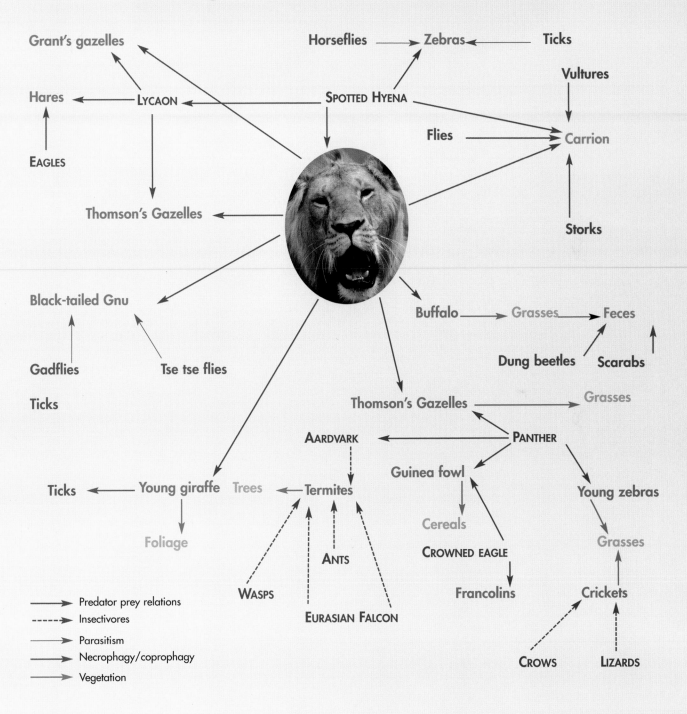

Grant's gazelles

Horseflies → Zebras ← Ticks

Vultures

Hares ← LYCAON ← SPOTTED HYENA

Flies → Carrion

EAGLES

Storks

Thomson's Gazelles

Black-tailed Gnu

Buffalo → Grasses → Feces

Gadflies

Tse tse flies

Dung beetles   Scarabs

Ticks

Grasses

Thomson's Gazelles → Grasses

AARDVARK ← PANTHER

Ticks ← Young giraffe   Trees ← Termites

Guinea fowl

Young zebras

Foliage

Cereals

Grasses

ANTS

CROWNED EAGLE

WASPS

Francolins   Crickets

EURASIAN FALCON

CROWS   LIZARDS

→ Predator prey relations
⇢ Insectivores
→ Parasitism
→ Necrophagy/coprophagy
→ Vegetation

# Description

The lion's coat is close-cropped with little variation in color. It runs from yellowish buff to brownish red, with its belly a lighter shade, sometimes almost white. At the extremity of its tail is a large tuft of hair, which sometimes conceals a small bone spur (only 2 inches long). Its ears are small and round. The male lion's mane begins to grow in its second year of life. Of varying length, it covers the head, neck and shoulders, as well as part of the chest. There are clear differences from one region to another. The now-vanished Barbary lion of North Africa had the longest mane; it extended to its stomach. Some male lions have no manes and occasionally females will sport little ones. It reaches its fullest dimensions when the lion is 5 to 6 years old.

Some lions have quite dark coats (a tendency toward melanism), whereas the coats of others are very light. The rare white lion has a coat that is not fully pigmented, but its skin and eyes are of normal color; so here it is the abnormality referred to as leucism, rather than albinoism, which denotes the complete absence of pigmentation. Leucism in lions has

Right: *Compared to smaller felines, big cats walk with their bellies rather close to the ground.*

Following spread, left: *The sparse whiskers of the lion have a tactile function; they are sensitive to vibrations, pressure, and contact.*

Following spread, right: *The lion's mane is composed of some dark hair as well as some hair of the same shade as the rest of his coat. The fullness of the mane varies between individuals and regions.*

been recorded near the Kruger National Park and the Umfolozi Reserve (both in South Africa). In 1997, two white cubs were born on the Timbavati Reserve (northwest of Johannesburg). They grew up without apparent difficulty, and without being rejected by the other pride members. Being brought along on the hunt by lionesses, they were easily spotted by the prospective prey and caused the hunters to come up empty. At the end of two years, one of the dominant males of the pride disappeared, and the cubs and their mother were forced out of the pride. Finally located, they were captured and brought to a zoo in Pretoria.

Adult lions measure from 4.5 to 6 feet in length, their tails adding another 2 to 3 feet. Lionesses are a little smaller (not including their tails , 4 to 5.5 feet). The males' weight ranges from 250 to 440 pounds, though 550 pounds has been reported. Lionesses weigh between 175 and 250 pounds. Their height at the shoulder ranges from 2.5 to 4 feet. The adult lion has 30 teeth.

A lion cub weighs about 3 pounds at birth and measures a foot in length, a quarter of which is its tail. Its eyes are closed at birth and open at 6 to 9 days old. Its coat is usually a light buff color with stripes and dark spots that seem to help camouflage it in high grass, when it stays still. It suckles for 4 to 6 months, but begins to eat small pieces of meat at 2 months, which constitutes its primary source of nourishment by 4 months. It grows slowly: at 6 weeks, its average weight is 8 to 15 pounds; at 6 months, somewhere between 40 and 50 pounds; at 15 months, perhaps 110 pounds. It starts to get around on its own after 3 weeks. If it escapes the numerous dangers that threaten the life of the lion cub, it can hope to live for up to 15 years in the wild (30 years in captivity).

Left: *Cats' tongues are raspy. They are covered with little bumps that help scrape meat from bones.*

Facing page: *Portrait of a lion cub. Like adult lions, it has small ears and a big nose.*

# Typical Habitat in the Savannah

In tropical Africa the lion lives in humid and dry savannahs. They can also be found in semi-arid environments. They like open country, with vegetation consisting primarily of herbaceous plants, and only scattered trees and shrubs. They do not inhabit the dense rainforests of the Congo, Gabon, and Zaire. The eastern savannah is characterized by wet and dry seasons. The great herds migrate during the dry seasons. In Somali and Tanzania there are two wet seasons: one commencing in May and the other at the end of October. The average temperature between October and March is 85°F, but daily temperatures can vary significantly and the air is less humid than in the forests. The savannahs are very rich in different kinds of animals: in Tanzania 45 species of herbivores and 41 species of carnivores have been counted. Lions are an integral part of the biotope in which they live. The ecosystems in which they live vary in temperature, topography, climate, soil, and so forth. The lions of the Kalahari clearly live in a very different environment from that of the lions of the Serengeti.

Everywhere species have adapted to the unique qualities their environment presents, tailoring their behavior, diet, their entire way of life to existing conditions. The totality of biological diversity forms a unity: the ecological niche in which an animal finds itself. This holds true for lions and the other animals with which it shares its world.

Facing page: *Remaining immobile, this lion blends into the background.*

Below: *Like the domestic cat, of which it is often reminiscent, the lion likes to roll on the ground and sleeps with its belly in the air in a state of total relaxation.*

Following spread: *It looks like this lion is playing hide-and-seek.*

# A Social Animal

The lion is a sociable animal, living as part of a pride whose importance is measured by the number of lionesses that it comprises. They are the permanent members of the group. One study of a pride found that one of the lionesses lived 15 years in the group, during which time 7 males came and went.

A pride of lions will stay in the same area for a long time. In the Serengeti three prides were observed occupying the same territory for more than 20 years. Prides' sizes vary widely. Again in the Serengeti, one pride comprised 2 dominant males, 13 lionesses and 20 cubs. In South Africa, some prides have been observed with only one dominant male, whereas others have had as many as 6. A single male in charge of a pride stays with it on average for a year.

Left: *Lionesses are the key members of their prides.*

Below: *The fully grown male could easily swallow this young cub.*

If there are 2 males, they may remain for up to 18 months. In prides with 4 or 6 dominant males, they have been known to stay for 4 to 8 years, the maximum being about 10 years.

In the Kalahari prides are smaller: the average number of lionesses per pride is 2.2, although prides with 4 to 6 lionesses are frequently seen, and in a time of great abundance of game, a pride made up of 20 lionesses was observed. Here members of prides are closely related since the young as a general rule remain within their pride of origin and interbreed. Thus the members are all mothers, daughters, sisters, cousins, and aunts. This is less the case in the Serengeti, where up to a third of a pride's members will leave the pride and strike out on their own.

Young males generally leave their pride sometime between the ages of 2 and 4—sometimes younger, at 13 to 20 months, when the pride is taken over by one or more males from the outside, who chase away their aging sire and take his place. In South Africa dominant males within the same clan are often related to one another but not to the lionesses. While lionesses protect their young, the males will defend the pride's territory, driving off other prides or solitary wandering males. They mark the boundaries of their territory with olfactory traces (urine, feces) and through their roars, which as we have seen carry great distances. Since

Above: *By playing with their siblings and other young members of the pride, cubs exercise their muscles and gain self-assurance. Some games simulate hunting and capturing prey, clear evidence of an apprenticeship that will serve them later in life.*

Below: *A young male lion whose mane is just beginning to come in. It will get darker as he grows older.*

territories can overlap, conflicts between rival males often occur. Rivals will strike each other with their claws, bite, and sometimes deal mortal wounds. The guardian males also have to be on the lookout for young unaffiliated males seeking to establish themselves within a pride. In the Kalahari one sees bands of 3 or 4 young males who look for prides with only a single male, whom they can overmaster. If a pride is defended by more than one male, they go elsewhere.

## Thinning the pride

Once an alien male (or males) takes over a pride, he searches out the hiding places of lionesses with very young cubs and kills the young. With the death of her young the lioness goes into heat and can bring the offspring of her new champion into the world. This binds the male close to the pride. This pattern of eliminating a part of the pride works as a measure of population control, so that the pride maintains a balance with its environment.

Within a pride both males and females enjoy each other's company, especially during the heat of the day when they relax together. They communicate with growls. Lions, unlike other great cats, also like to climb trees, no doubt to get away from insects and parasites and to take advantage of any passing breeze. It is mainly lionesses and cubs who engage in tree climbing, as they are lighter and more agile than the

Below: *A lion cub is not always closely supervised by its mother. It may leave its hiding place when she goes out to hunt. Its coat remains spotted until it is about a year old. Adult males sometimes have dark patches on their coats, but only on their paws and bellies.*

Above and right: *Distancing themselves from the rest of the pride, the lion and lioness live together for a few days during which they couple frequently.*

males. This behavior has been frequently observed in the Lake Manyara Reserve (in East Africa).

The lion's walking gait is slow, around 2.5 miles per hour. They can easily jump to heights of 10 feet and leap distances of over 30 feet.

## Reproduction

Lions are polygamous. In South Africa lionesses go into heat from two to four times every two years, if they rear their cubs until they are fully weaned. They become sexually receptive in the month that their young leave; they give off an odor that signals their receptivity to the males of the pride. One of the males will then follow her; no others attempt to interfere. There is no rivalry for females between males of the

same pride, but the pride members will kill an intruder who tries to mate with one of their lionesses. The male lion who follows the female pulls back his upper lip, facilitating the perception of his vomeronasal organ (Jacobson's organ), an important component of his olfactory system. At the same time he opens his throat, closes his nostrils and raises his head. This behavior was identified by German ethologists, who named it the flehmen response.

Either the male or the female can initiate sexual activity. The female demonstrates her receptivity by rubbing herself against the male or lying down beside him. Acts of intercourse are brutal and frequent (often four times per hour over a period of one or two days, although each lasts less than a minute). When it is

Above: *A lioness suckling her cub.*

over the male will bite the female once or twice on the neck and the partners will roll around the ground together, licking and rubbing each other. If the male tires and the female is still in heat she may approach another male. Gestation lasts on average 110 days (ranging from 100 to 114 days).

## Birth and child rearing
In a large pride births are often closely synchronized. Cubs are raised by all of the lionesses in the community. Any lactating female will suckle them. Lionesses

first give birth at about 5 years old. Newborn cubs are kept in a shelter some distance from the rest of the pride, and the lionesses will move them to another hiding place if the group is under threat.

When they are about 2 months old, the cubs are brought back to live together with the rest of the pride. Male cubs will remain for several years; females will live with the pride all their lives. Lions have four teats, but they generally bear litters three or less. If there are more than four cubs in a litter (the most being six), it may happen that not all of them survive. The biologist B.C.R. Bertram, who has closely studied the social life of lions, has reported an interval of seven months in which no cubs were born. This happened following the deposition of the dominant males by a group of strangers. After that there were several births, offspring of the new leaders. When the cubs were presented to their fellows (after their first month's retreat) the males adopted them into the pride.

*Above right and left: Any lioness within a pride will take care of cubs. They do not have to be her own for her to suckle, groom, or watch over them.*

*Right: In the wild, lions' coats are often torn or damaged by thorny shrubs and other vegetation.*

# Students of the African Lion

Before biologists began to make a close study of the behavior of lions in the second half the twentieth century, most information about their way of life in the wild was provided by hunters, many of whom were careful observers. The majority of recent studies have taken place in national parks and reserves. Among the most important scientific studies are those of C.A.W. Guggisberg (1961) and G. Schaller (1972). Schaller's work is particularly noteworthy. In addition to his studies of lions, he has written on mountain gorillas, tigers in India, the great Pandas of China, and finally the ungulates of the high plateaus of Tibet. Schaller spent three years observing the lions of Tanzania. He tagged 150 individuals after anesthetizing them from a distance and installed some with miniature tracking devices. A lion quickly recovers from anesthesia, raising its head after 3 minutes and getting up on its feet within 15 minutes. He followed the lions in the Serengeti over a territory of 50 square miles, and observed 14 prides each with 2 or 3 males and 2 to 12 adults females (plus cubs). B.C.R.

Bertram spent time in the Serengeti between 1966 and 1973, following two prides. He provided a comprehensive description of the behavior of young male lions. The German naturalist and ethologist V. B. Dröscher also observed lions (and many other species as well). Last but not least, one should not forget the determinative role of the former director of the Frankfurt Zoo, B. Grzimek, who forcefully argued for the conservation of African wildlife.

Facing page: *This gives a clear picture of the lion's small incisors: six above and six below, neatly framed by its large canines.*

Below left: *The head of the lion cub is not as round as that of an adult lion.*

Below right: *In national parks with their tourists and rangers, lions become accustomed to the presence of people and their vehicles.*

# The Asiatic Lion

The Asiatic lion is a little smaller than its African cousin: the male is about 8 feet long, the female perhaps 7.5 feet (including the tail). It also has a shorter mane. It lives in the Gir Forest (1,000 square miles, of which 160 is national park) and the surrounding area. The forest is dry and in part formed of teak trees. People there raise livestock, which has become the source of many conflicts. Lions are being forced out of the forest because their population has become too dense. This has inspired plans to create another reserve.

About a third of the prey of these lions are domestic animals. In addition they hunt sambar and chital deer.

Completely isolated, the Asiatic lion is threatened by the genetic disadvantages of inbreeding as well as the extension of cultivated lands and increasing human population. Its total number has varied over the past decades. There were 287 in 1937, 177 in 1968, and 284 in 1990 (99 males, 122 females, and 63 cubs). The last census (in 1995) recorded 304 lions.

Facing page: *African lion.*

Below: *Asiatic lion* (Panthera leo persica).

# Man Eaters

Compared to the tiger, the lion is much less of a man eater. This arises in part from the fact that the human population density in Asia is much greater than that of Africa. Among the best known cases was one in 1898, when about 140 workers on a bridge across the Tsavo River in Kenya were killed in the space of nine months. These workers slept in open tents; it seems they were attacked because to feed themselves they had hunted down the lion's customary prey. In 1925 in Uganda, two lions killed 124 people.

Today lions generally will not attack tourists who sleep in closed tents. But it is imprudent to sleep out in the open in a sleeping bag or to have savory food in one's tent (even if it is closed).

Man eaters are generally solitary lions, although between 1900 and 1910 one pride killed ten people in South Africa. And threats do not come only from old or feeble lions: in Kruger National Park a hungry lioness killed five people in two days. Hunger often drives such attacks. In some localities human activities have driven away the lion's natural prey, so they turn to humans as a substitute.

Facing page: *As a general rule, lions have better success hunting at night, especially if the moon is not bright.*

Below: *It feels good to stretch.*

# Tigers

➤ *Page 6*: Along with the jaguar, the tiger is the most magnificent of the big cats.

➤ *Page 74*: Everything about the tiger speaks of suppleness and power.

➤ *Page 76*: A fine representative of the breed in an Indian nature preserve.

➤ *Page 76*: Portrait of a phantom that will soon be seen only in captivity: the magnificent Bengal tiger.

➤ *Page 77*: This tiger displays its impressive canine teeth.

➤ *Pages 78–79*: In their Indian nature preserve, young tigers have the opportunity to lead peaceful lives, though given the relentless demographic pressure, it is not certain for how long.

➤ *Page 80*: Tiger habitats

➤ *Page 81*: Tigers love water. Zoos that have tigers need to ensure that they have an adequate supply.

➤ *Pages 82–83*: Living in a vast enclosure where it can find part of its accustomed biotope, this tiger is in perfect health. The snow does not disturb it in the least.

➤ *Page 84*: Finding a gap in the ice, a tiger drinks cool fresh water, a true delicacy in frigid eastern Siberia.

➤ *Page 85*: While its Siberian cousin loves the cold, the Bengal tiger thrives in hotter climates, as long as there is shade to protect it and an ample supply of water.

➤ *Pages 86–87*: Tigers are solitary animals rarely friendly to their fellows; the exception is with its mate, toward whom it can evince great tenderness.

➤ *Pages 88–89*: The cold invigorates the Siberian tiger. As this photograph shows, it enjoys the snow.

➤ *Page 90*: To survive, the tiger requires a vast heavily forested territory with easy access to water and abundant large game. Along with the jaguar, the tiger is the most aquatic of all the cats.

➤ *Page 91*: Siberian tiger in its winter coat.

➤ **Page 92:** The tiger's sumptuous coat encourages poaching to fulfill the wishes of greedy, unscrupulous, and foolish people. Today twice as many tigers live in captivity as remain in the wild.

➤ **Page 93:** This tiger is on its way to a refreshing bath

➤ **Pages 94–95:** « A tigress at ease with her cub. But she does not relax her constant vigilance, since her young is vulnerable to attacks from males encroaching on her territory

➤ **Page 96:** The male tiger roams over a wide territory, visiting his mates living within its boundaries and defending it from intruders.

➤ **Page 96:** The male tiger roams over a wide territory, visiting his mates living within its boundaries and defending it from intruders.

➤ **Page 97:** This tiger's peaceful yawn shows its impressive jaws, the most powerful of all cats.

➤ **Pages 98–99:** The rarity of the white tiger led it to be included in the retinue of princes and maharajahs, who were unaware that its unusual coloration was a result of a genetic deficiency, leucism.

➤ **Page 100:** A Siberian tiger couple preparing to mate. The male, on the right, has more luxuriant whiskers than the female.

➤ **Page 101:** No matter the latitude of their habitats, tigers seek out areas with heavy vegetation and a lot of water.

➤ **Page 101:** Tiger in a game park in India.

➤ **Page 102–103:** From a distance, the tiger's striped coat is perfect camouflage, particularly when the tiger lies in high grass.

➤ **Page 104:** A Bengal tiger in a zoo especially built for him

➤ **Page 105:** A Siberian tiger sporting his sumptuous winter coat

➤ **Page 105:** This Bengal tiger is seen strolling through its natural habitat in India.

➤ **Page 106:** Like all felines, the tiger marks his territory in different ways, notably by scratching the trunks of trees, much as a house cat scratches the legs of chairs and tables.

➤ **Page 107:** A Siberian tiger in captivity. Does it enjoy having nothing to do, or does it long for its vast lost territories?

# Portfolio of Tigers

> **Pages 108–109:** This magnificent Siberian tiger has just left an olfactory mark on the trunk of a fallen tree, as betrayed by his uplifted, curved tail.

> **Page 110:** A gaur *(Bos gaurus)*.

> **Page 110:** A sambar deer *(Cervus unicolor)*.

> **Page 111:** Well-camouflaged in the underbrush, the tiger is on the lookout for its favorite prey, gaur or deer.

> **Page 112:** A tiger stalking its prey in high grass is practically invisible. By the time it makes its presence known, it is usually too late for its prey to escape.

> **Page 113:** Tranquilly resting on a rocky promontory, this young tiger seems to be enjoying its continuing discovery of the world around it, as evidenced by its attentive and curious gaze.

> **Page 114:** The tiger's preferred gait is a fast walk. It can only run flat out for short distances and rarely exceeds 30 miles per hour. (The lion's top speed can reach 50 miles per hour.)

> **Page 114:** Like most large predators, whether mammals, reptiles or fish, tigers know how to use their energy in the most economical fashion. This is essential for animals that hunt large prey.

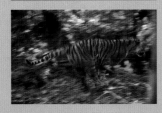

> **Page 114:** Like most large predators, whether mammals, reptiles or fish, tigers know how to use their energy in the most economical fashion. This is essential for animals that hunt large prey.

> **Page 115:** Young love: two Siberian tigers.

> **Pages 116–117:** The tiger is not a sociable animal, except for brief periods of mating during which the couple shares their territory.

> **Page 118:** The preliminaries are now over—preparing the female for intercourse is their primary aim—but that fact does not rule out displays of deep tenderness.

> **Page 119:** Exploring the world, the young tiger proceeds at a gallop.

> **Page 119:** This tiger was afraid of the photographer.

> **Pages 120–121:** This still clumsy young tiger calls for its mother. What chance for survival does human folly allow it?

> **Page 122:** Bengal tiger. It is estimated that the 10,000 tigers in captivity in the United States is double the total number of tigers in the wild.

➤ *Page 123*: A number of private individuals own one or more tigers. But the tiger is not a domestic animal. Since 1990, captive tigers have killed 11 people and injured more than 60.

➤ *Pages 124–125*: Handicapped by the loss of its canine teeth, this tiger would no doubt attack humans, who are easy if not preferred prey. This condemns it to death unless it has the good fortune to live in a nature preserve.

➤ *Pages 126–127*: This Siberian tiger lives in his natural environment in a preserve. For how long? The tiger's end is quickly approaching despite international measures to protect it. Its territories too often abut areas with burgeoning human populations. Interspecies encounters all to often become conflicts in which the tiger is the inevitable loser.

It is sad to reflect that the Five Tigers soon will be found only in captivity, wiped out by our heedlessness.

# Introduction

Along with the jaguar, the tiger is the most magnificent of the big cats, and it is not simply chance that accounts for its marked similarities with certain Chinese and Pre-Columbian myths. On one side of the Pacific, the Five Tigers are the guardians of the four cardinal points and the center. They are considered warriors, guardians of the empire. Across the ocean, according to Mayan mythology, the Four Jaguars watch over and protect the four cardinal points, the ways into the village and the maize fields. The Aztecs considered the jaguar to be emblematic of the warrior caste. This cultural convergence is hardly surprising in that both animals are nocturnal, powerful, unpredictable, and beautiful. Both are fascinating and provoke fear and admiration—fitting subjects for foundation myths.

In our time they have the tragic fate of being well on the way to extinction. The great naturalist, Paul Géraudet, some time ago noted: "The incompatibility of [the tiger] and human concerns leave little hope for their continuing survival, failing the establishment of national parks under strict supervision that encompass an adequate area of favorable habitat—these measures need to be supplemented with strict controls on hunting inside and outside of these protected areas" (*Animaux en peril*, Lausanne, 1970).

We are going to see the extent to which these recommendations have been ignored. Let us follow what may well be the last footsteps of the these great creatures in the wild.

# The Tiger's World

### True and False Ancestors

To say straight out that tigers are carnivores will not come as news to any of our readers. To add that, within the order of carnivores, they are part of the family Felidae narrows our focus a little. Within this family there are two subfamilies, felis and caracal. The former includes big and small cats (from the puma to the domestic cat as well as the lynx), the latter is reserved for the caracal cat, which is similar to the lynx. Identified as big cats are the lion, tiger, jaguar, and panther (all part of the genus *Panthera*), the leopard (genus *Acionyx*), and the clouded leopard (genus *Neofelis*).

All true and false cats share a common ancestor that first appeared toward the end of the Paleocene era, between 50 and 60 million years ago. This progenitor resembled a kind of small weasel, the miacis, at most 15 inches long. This species disappeared at the beginning of the Oligocene era, but not before dividing into four major branches, of which the last was that of the Felidae. Around this time, about 30 million years ago, the ancestor of all of today's cats arose, the Proailarus, which was then followed by the Pseudaelurus, which produced two branches. The first was the Machairodonts, saber-toothed tigers, which became extinct about ten thousand years ago. The second branch is the Felidae (as well as Neofelidae), through the intermediary of the genus *Scizalarius*.

Members of this genus are the direct ancestors of the cats of the genus *Felis*, which came into existence

Below left: *A fine representative of the breed in an Indian nature preserve.*

Below right: *Portrait of a phantom that will soon be seen only in captivity: the magnificent Bengal tiger. Note its impressive canines, shown on the facing page.*

about 12 million years ago. Out of this genus came the puma, leopard, and lynx (respectively, 8.5, 7, and 6.7 million years ago). Last to appear was the genus *Panthera*, to which belongs the tiger. Beyond that, direct fossil evidence is lacking to pinpoint the differentiation of each species of *Panthera*. Or to put it another way, the direct descendants of the tiger, lion, and panther have been lost in the mist of a prehistoric time that is, relatively speaking, not so distant from today. One can, however, note that the evolution of the carnivores was slow to begin with and then quickened as the different species of cats came into existence. It took only 6 million years for the various species to distinguish themselves from their common ancestor, a sort of record in biological evolution.

Insofar as the saber-toothed tigers are concerned, those of the genus *Machairodon* lived in Africa and Europe, and those of the genus *Smilodon* lived in the Americas. Just to set the record straight, neither of these were ancestors of today's cats (whether big or small).

## Real tigers

The tiger (*Panthera tigris*) is found only in Asia. (Contrary to the mistaken idea fostered by extravagant accounts of early mariners and explorers, there are no African tigers.) They are comprised of one species, which relatively recently divided into eight subspecies, of which three met with extinction over the course of forty years in the twentieth century (1940–1980). The five remaining subspecies are all threatened with a similar fate. They have all been placed upon the protected list of CITES, the Convention on International Trade in Endangered Species). The tiger is without doubt the most severely threatened animal in the

*In their Indian nature preserve, young tigers have the opportunity to lead peaceful lives, though given the relentless demographic pressure, it is not certain for how long.*

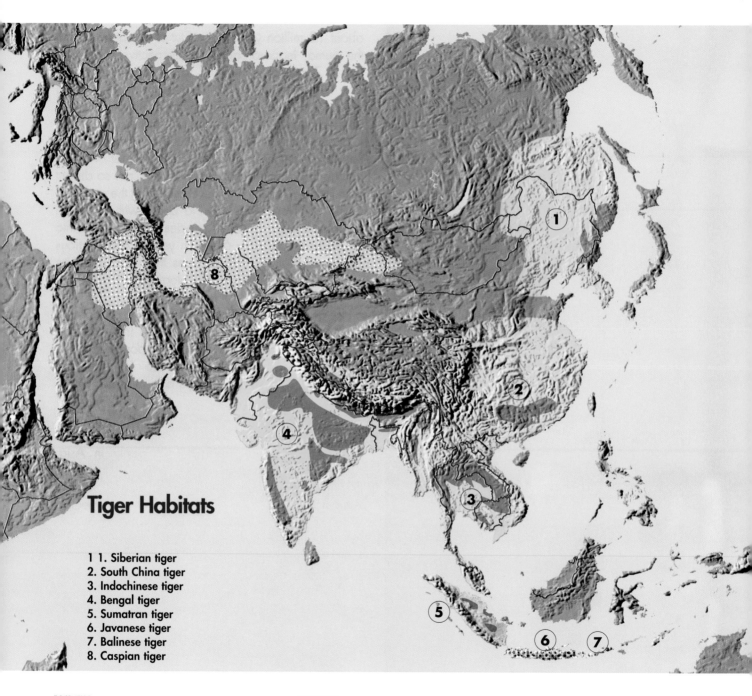

# Tiger Habitats

1 1. Siberian tiger
2. South China tiger
3. Indochinese tiger
4. Bengal tiger
5. Sumatran tiger
6. Javanese tiger
7. Balinese tiger
8. Caspian tiger

 Former habitats    Current habitats-

world, even more than the extremely rare blue whale. The situation is so dire that writing this very modest study posed the problem of whether to use the present or past tense—to know whether one is evoking a living, breathing being or a ghost. So it is with sorrow and anger that we enter the world of this splendid animal.

## Red list, black list

What follows are the findings reported in the International Union for the Conservation of Nature and Natural Resources (IUCN) Red List of Threatened Species to summarize the current status of the tiger. It constitutes a black list of human activities.

### Caspian tiger (*Panthera tigris virgata*)

Territory: Southwest Asia around the Caspian and Aral Seas and from Iraq to China.

Status: Extinct from the beginning of the 1970s.

Causes: Hunting and competition from human activities, as well as the destruction of habitat and the disappearance of the large animals upon which it preyed.

Presence in captivity: None.

### Balinese tiger (*Panthera tigris balica*)

Territory: Bali (Indonesia).

Status: Became extinct between 1930 and 1970.

Causes: Hunting, destruction of forest, and disappearance of prey, combined with the increase of human population on the island.

Presence in captivity: None.

### Javan tiger (*Panthera tigris sondaica*)

Territory: Java (Indonesia).

Status: Extinct from the beginning of the 1980s. The last observation of a Javan tiger dates from 1976 in Java's sole remaining nature preserve, Meru Betiri, on the southeast coast. In the nineteenth century the tiger population was spread throughout the island, but in 1950 the population had diminished to 25 individuals.

Causes: Mainly hunting and deforestation. Its decline within a protected area resulted from a lack of prey, particularly of Cervidae (true deer).

Presence in captivity: None.

### Sumatran tiger (*Panthera tigris sumatrae*)

Territory: Sumatra (Indonesia).

Status: Critical. In great danger of extinction; the current population numbers no more than 250 and is declining rapidly. No subpopulation comprises more than 50 reproductive adults.

Causes: Widespread poaching and destruction of natural habitat by human encroachment.

Presence in captivity: About 210.

### South China tiger (*Panthera tigris amoyensis*), also known as the Amoy tiger.

Territory: South China in the regions of Hunan, Fujian, Guangdong, and Jiangxi. Originally inhabiting the east,

*Tigers love water. Zoos that have tigers need to ensure that they have an adequate supply.*

center, and south of the country (to the 40th parallel), its current name emphasizes its precarious position.

Status: Critical. In great danger of extinction. Its current population is estimated at 20 to 80 individuals. After deliberate massacres were halted, the population began to increase gradually, but it is now in decline once more on account of continued hunting and poaching; only one preserve offers them protection. According to some authors, it may now be too late for them to survive in the wild.

Causes: Exclusively, the criminal stupidity of Chinese authorities. The tiger was declared a "harmful pest" in 1950 by an irresponsible government. Its extermination, pure and simple, was ordered and systematically pursued. Bowing to international pressure, the Chinese government outlawed tiger hunting in 1979. From a population of about 4,000 in 1950, the count has dwindled to as few as 20, which is effectively none at all.

Presence in captivity: About 47 distributed through the 18 zones of the country. This is not enough to preserve the race. The current Chinese government has committed itself to the task, but it seems that its efforts are too late; there are not enough individuals to ensure its survival. An attempt was made to readapt a breeding couple into a special farm in South Africa with the hope of ultimately reintroducing them into their native habitat in China, but the enterprise seemed doomed as the male sickened and died of an infectious disease.

### Siberian tiger (*Panthera tigris altaica*)

Territory: Siberia, Manchuria, and the extreme north of North Korea. In earlier times it roamed from Lake Baikal to Lena and to the basins of Oussouri and

*Living in a vast enclosure where it can find part of its accustomed biotope, this tiger is in perfect health. The snow does not disturb it in the least.*

Amour, venturing into South Korea.

Status: Critical. Along with the South China tiger, it is the subspecies most in danger of extinction, despite spotty efforts at protection. As of 2001, its population of reproductive adults numbered no more than 250 dispersed over a shrinking and discontinuous territory.

Causes: Widespread hunting, accompanied by the destruction of forests, which continue to be exploited. It is important to bear in mind that Russian forests are disappearing almost as quickly as the Amazon jungle. Only 20 percent of tigers in Russia dwell in protected areas where poaching is combated. Outside of these areas, tigers fall victim to poachers who hunt them for their fur as well as for ingredients used in traditional Chinese medicine. They are also hunted for the trade in endangered species, a practice that only intensifies as their numbers decrease.

Presence in captivity: There are two and a half times as many Siberian tigers in captivity as in the wild: about 1,000 compared with 400.

### Indochinese tiger *(Panthera tigris corbetti)*

Territory: Southeast Asia, from Burma to South China, passing through Thailand (where it is most numerous), Cambodia, Vietnam, and the Malaysian Peninsula.

Status: Threatened. The population, which is spread over a vast area, continues to decline. Current figures are between 1,200 and 1,700.

Causes: Its habitats are discontinuous, with a lack of prey in some areas, and it has to compete with an increasing human population. To these factors must be added political instability in many of the countries it inhabits, which does not inspire confidence in the their willingness or ability to abide by international treaties and conventions.

Presence in captivity: About 60 in Asian and American zoos.

### Bengal tiger *(Panthera tigris tigris)*

Territory: The Bengal tiger has the widest range of any of the subspecies of tiger. It is found in the center, north, and southwest of India as well as in Bhutan, western Burma, and South China.

Above: *Although its Siberian cousin loves the cold, the Bengal tiger thrives in hotter climates, as long as there is shade to protect it and an ample supply of water.*

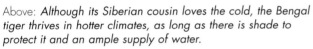

Facing page : *Finding a gap in the ice, a tiger drinks cool fresh water, a true delicacy in frigid eastern Siberia.*

Status: In danger. Although it has the widest range and the largest population, it is not protected outside of scattered preserves where safeguards are not always sufficiently strict. It is estimated that there are about 2,500 reproductive adults in a total population of 3,000–4,000. But the trend is toward a decline in numbers despite protective measures taken mainly in India. (The IUCN has recently called upon the Prime Minister of India to guarantee that he will follow the laws of his own country.)

Causes: Illegal hunting, threats from various directions, fragmentation of territory, poaching in protected areas, deforestation, disappearance of the prey upon which the tiger depends, and the expansion and increase of human population leading to encounters that often end with the death of the animals. The commercial motivation to supply ingredients for traditional Chinese medicine remains strong, despite the sincere efforts of the Chinese government to find chemical substitutes for a pharmacology that has such a destructive impact.

Presence in captivity: 350 primarily in zoos in India.

From the foregoing it is clear that that three subspecies have been lost forever; the lack of any specimens in captivity allows us no hope that they

can be once again introduced into the wild. One subspecies lived in a closely circumscribed island environment with a growing human population, and the other two were relentlessly hunted and unable to resist the destruction of their marshland environment. Of the surviving subspecies, the South China tiger may be able to survive if heroic measures are taken; the Siberian tiger is on the verge of extinction; and the lot of the Sumatran tiger is not much more promising. As to the Bengal and Indochinese tigers, their chances worsen with each passing year.

Although it is difficult to conceive of the extinction of a race of animals, whatever it may be, that is spread out over a wide territory, it is unfortunately much easier to envisage the destruction of island-dwelling species. With a surface area of 2,200 square miles and 3 million inhabitants, Bali has a population density of almost 1,400 people per square mile. Java has a population density of almost 2,400 people per square mile, with a population of 120 million inhabitants spread over 51,000 square miles. As for the Sumatran tiger, the relatively sparse human population has allowed it to remain the last survivor in the Indonesian archipelago.

In short, the list is red with the blood of tigers and black with human folly. The numbers speak for themselves.

Left: *Tigers are solitary animals rarely friendly to their fellows; the exception is its mate, toward whom it can evince great tenderness.*

Following pages: *The cold invigorates the Siberian tiger. As this photograph shows, it enjoys the snow.*

## Themes

Like nearly all cats, the tiger is a carnivore with digitigrade feet and retractile claws. (The cheetah is the only exception. Its claws do not retract.) The tiger has powerful jaws armed with impressive canine teeth, small incisors, and pointed molars designed to tear rather than chew. One need only watch a dog or cat eat a large piece of meat to see that they do not chew their food. They tear it, mash it a little bit to reduce it to a more manageable size, and transform it into pulp that they can swallow. Unsympathetic observers claim to descry an expression of savagery or gluttony, but this is a anthropomorphic misinterpretation, since cats, both big and small, are made to eat in this fashion. In all fairness, however, one can understand how the tiger might be viewed in this way, as they are perfectly capable of tearing a person to pieces. This capacity has led to its being pursued and hunted down without mercy whenever it finds itself in close proximity to human population, which is to say almost everywhere, with the exception of Siberia. And even there it is being pushed to the brink of extinction.

Its coat is of a more or less dark orange color on the back, flanks, underneath its head, and paws, and is white on the inner surfaces of its legs and neck. Vertical black stripes (sometimes doubled) run around its body and join up in a V shape to make an elegant collar when the animal is lying down. Its long and supple tail is sometimes white, but more often orange above and white underneath, always ringed in black. Its eyebrows, cheeks, chops, and chin are white, its ears small and round, and its pink snout sometimes touched with black. Its body is long and supple. Its powerful paws leave six-inch prints on the ground, and its sharply curved claws can measure four inches

*To survive, the tiger requires a vast heavily forested territory with easy access to water and abundant large game. Along with the jaguar, the tiger is the most aquatic of all the cats.*

in length. Its hind legs are longer than its forelegs, enabling powerful leaps of 20 to 30 feet. Its round head with yellow eyes ends in powerful jaws. Under its sumptuous coat one can make out an extremely well-developed musculature. In all, the tiger evokes undeniable force and suppleness. Its chest, however, is relatively weak in comparison to its near relation, the lion, and its more distant cousin, the leopard, which means that it is not a champion runner. This is hardly a disadvantage since it relies upon strength and agility to succeed as a hunter. Despite minor variations, all of the subspecies of tiger are built along these lines.

## Variations

From a distance, even when they stand close together (in zoos or parks, for example) all tigers resemble one another. However, upon more careful observation, one perceives that they are all different. Most obvious is differences in size. Their height at the shoulder ranges from 1.5 to 2 feet, their length between 3.5 to 7 feet. The color of their coats varies, some darker, some brighter, and the appearance of their stripes differs widely even in individuals of the same subspecies. These variations are understandable given the immense breadth of their original territory and the dif-

*Siberian tiger in its winter coat.*

*The tiger's sumptuous coat encourages poaching to fulfill the wishes of greedy, unscrupulous, and foolish people. Today twice as many tigers live in captivity as remain in the wild.*

fering biotopes in which they have resided—from the confines of western Asia where the Romans captured them for their circuses to the Arctic Circle and far eastern parts and tropics of Asia. Let us survey the different types of tigers, from west to east and north to south. (Note that lengths are given from the tip of the nose to the end of the tail.)

## Caspian tiger, in memory only, since it has been extinct since 1970.

Weight of the male: 360 to 500 pounds

Weight of the female: 190 to 300 pounds
Length of male: 8 to 10 feet
Length of female: 7 to 8 feet
One of the largest of the subspecies, scarcely smaller than the Bengal tiger, it was distinguished by its long whiskers, its bold stripes, its very white chest, and its long and abundant winter coat.

## Siberian tiger

Weight of the male: 400 to 660 pounds (The heaviest tiger recorded was 800 pounds for an animal killed in 1950.)
Weight of the female: 220 to 375 pounds
Length of male: 8 to 11 feet
Length of female: 7 to 8.5 feet
With these dimensions the Siberian tiger is not only

the largest of all tigers, it is the largest and most powerful of all of the big cats. (By comparison, a large lion can reach 11 feet in length but rarely weighs more than 500 pounds.) Its winter coat is very thick, paler than the coats of other tigers. Its stripes are lighter, rather brown than black. Its neck is furnished with a thick collar, and the throat of both sexes is larger than that of other subspecies. Its claws can reach 4 inches in length.

### South China tiger

Weight of the male: 280 to 385 pounds
Weight of the female: 220 to 250 pounds
Length of male: 7 to 8 feet
Length of female: 6.75 to 7.5 feet
This medium-sized cat has a deep orange coat with short stripes that are wider and more spaced out than its Siberian and Bengal cousins.

### Bengal tiger

Weight of the male: 400 to 575 pounds
Weight of the female: 220 to 350 pounds
Length of male: 8.25 to 9.5 feet
Length of female: 7.25 to 8 feet
The Bengal tiger is large and heavy. It wears a brown-orange coat with widely spaced stripes. Its forequarters are sometimes very lightly marked. It is classified quite simply as subspecies Panthera tigris tigris because it was the first subspecies described—by Linnaeus in 1758. Some researchers do not distinguish it from the Siberian tiger, judging the variations in the two types to be within the normal range for a subspecies. The other subspecies are all smaller and live in warmer climates. Zoologists suggest that hotter temperatures result in a diminution in size, a plausible theory when one looks at deer, bears, or wolves, as long as one does not equate reduced size with degeneracy.

*This tiger is on its way to a refreshing bath.*

### Indochinese tiger
Weight of the male: 330 to 430 pounds
Weight of the female: 220 to 285 pounds
Length of male: 7.5 to 8.25 feet
Length of female: 7 to 7.75 feet
This tiger is smaller than the Bengal tiger but larger than the South China tiger. The base of its coat is very deep orange with more delicate stripes than those of other subspecies.

### Sumatran tiger
Weight of the male: 220 to 300 pounds
Weight of the female: 165 to 250 pounds
Length of male: 6.75 to 7.75 feet
Length of female: 6.5 to 7 feet
The Sumatran tiger is one of the smallest tigers, a small female weighing little more than a male panther. It is found only in Sumatra. Its deep orange coat is set off with delicate stripes, sometimes double strips. Its belly is not as white as in other subspecies.

### Javan tiger (extinct ca. 1980)
Weight of the male: 220 to 300 pounds
Weight of the female: 165 to 250 pounds
Length of male: 7.25 feet
Length of female: (unknown)
The Javan tiger was very similar to the Sumatra tiger.

### Balinese tiger (extinct ca. 1940)
Weight of the male: 200 to 220 pounds
Weight of the female: 175 to 200 pounds
Length of male: 6.75 to 7 feet

*A tigress at ease with her cub. But she does not relax her constant vigilance, since her young is vulnerable to attacks from males encroaching on her territory.*

Length of female: 6 to 6.5 feet

The Balinese tiger was the smallest of all the tigers; it was the first to disappear. It is also the least well known. Since it was only classified as a subspecies in 1912 (Schwarz), no systematic study of it was ever undertaken. We possess only one photograph: hanging by it legs, killed by a proud hunter.

## The white tiger

Traditionally the appanage of princes and kings, a white variety of Bengal tiger appears from time to time. This sport of nature is in fact the result of a genetic defect that can cause serious morphological malformations, particularly in the face. Its chances of survival in the wild are not good.

The white tiger is not, however, an albino. One can make out black stripes in its fur, and its eyes are blue rather than an albino's red. At night and when excited

Left and below: *The male tiger roams over a wide territory, visiting his mates living within its boundaries and defending it from intruders.*

Facing page: *This tiger's peaceful yawn shows its impressive jaws, the most powerful of all cats.*

its eyes turn yellow. If it reaches adulthood, it can reproduce, but it is usually killed by its fellows when it is young. This may appear ruthless to sensitive souls, but there are in fact excellent evolutionary reasons for this behavior, since it protects the species from a genetic handicap that if transmitted could lead to degeneracy.

Nonetheless there are certain parks and zoos that look for specimens with this aberrant coloration (called leucism) for purely commercial reasons, since white tigers seem to attract more visitors. The tiger is not a domestic animal. Such practices raise questions about the ethics of preservation, especially since zoos and parks are now repositories of the genetic material of a species rapidly disappearing in the wild. We are referring here to responsible establishments that bar cross-breeding between subspecies in order to conserve the full range of the tiger genotype. Unfortunately there are only a few such places.

### Diverse habitats

The tiger has spread from its origins in Turkey to the tropical jungles of Indonesia, passing through the frigid climates of Siberia and the Himalayas. It is clearly a highly adaptive animal, encountered in a wide variety of biotopes. The Caspian tiger frequented river valleys filled with trees and shrubs, beds of dense and high reeds, and prairies with high grass. Other subspecies are found in the evergreen or caduceus forests of South and Southeast Asia, passing through the dry thorny forest of India, the taiga with its coniferous

*The rarity of the white tiger led it to be included in the retinue of princes and maharajahs, who were unaware that its unusual coloration was a result of a genetic deficiency, leucism. White adults are especially rare since they are at greater risk of being attacked and killed by other tigers, an evolutionary device to ensure the health of the species. Only Bengal tigers suffer from leucism. Scientists do not know why other subspecies are not affected by it.*

forests, and the birch forests of Siberia. Taking advantage of dense vegetal ground cover, it has evolved from the 6,000-foot-high plateaus in eastern Siberia to the 9,000-foot-high forests of South China. The Bengal tiger still resides in high Himalayan valleys and has been spotted at altitudes as high as 12,000 feet. At the other extreme, members of the same subspecies can be found in the mangrove forest of the Sundarbans, the immense tree-filled delta formed by the Ganges, Brahmaputra, and Meghna Rivers along the Bay of Bengal. The Indochinese tiger dwells in mangrove forests in Malaysia as well. (As a reminder, mangrove is one of three tropical forest types, characterized by these strange trees that survive with their roots in seawater.)

All subspecies of tiger enjoy swampy forests. The tiger is an excellent swimmer and does not hesitate to cross streams and rivers, even narrow bands of ocean, if the need arises.

## Necessary conditions

This vast range of inhabited territory through such diverse environments is certainly impressive. However, upon close observation, the variations are not as

*A Siberian tiger couple preparing to mate. The male, on the right, has more luxuriant whiskers than the female.*

great as they seem. It is true that the tiger has adapted to extreme ranges of temperature. But its needs are in fact quite inflexible, and the same no matter where it finds itself. Since it is a large predator, it can only thrive in environments that offer vast, heavy vegetation to conceal its eye-catching black stripes. Its habitats must also support a sufficient quality and quantity of prey to ensure its survival, primarily varieties of deer and swine. And finally, a sine qua non for its survival is a large amount of water. It needs water not only to quench its thirst, but also for bathing. The tiger (along with the jaguar) is the large cat most in love with water. It can pass hours on end in the heat of the day submerged in rivers or salt marshes. The presence of humans does not in itself present a insurmountable hurdle, as long as encounters are kept to a minimum and its other basic needs (vegetation, supply of prey, and water) are provided for.

So its adaptability is limited to ravages in its environment that affect the availability of prey. Deprived of what it needs to survive, the tiger has disappeared from most of its previous territory. The individuals that do survive are a kind

Above and below: *Tigers in a game park in India. No matter the latitude of their habitats, tigers seek out areas with heavy vegetation and a lot of water.*

Following spread: *From a distance, the tiger's striped coat is perfect camouflage, particularly when the tiger lies in high grass.*

of walking ghost, given no more than a stay of execution. No matter how much their genes may want to adapt, there is simply not enough time for them to cope with the inexorable advance of human culture and its effects on the environment.

Right: *A Bengal tiger in a zoo especially built for him.*

Below: *This Bengal tiger is seen strolling through its natural habitat in India.*

Facing page: *A Siberian tiger sporting his sumptuous winter coat.*

# The Life of the Tiger

Except for lions, big cats are solitary animals who will at best tolerate the presence of their fellows. Tigers are no exception to this rule. Relations between males and females are at times cordial, even outside the context of mating. Same-sex relations are usually less friendly, ranging from chilly encounters to territorial conflicts between females to open warfare and pitched battles between males.

## Territory

Within a population of tigers, each individual establishes his or her own territory. The extent of the territory is determined by the sex of the tiger, the nature of the terrain, and the abundance of prey. Males insist upon a wider territory for themselves, the boundaries of which they strongly defend against incursions from other males. This exclusive territory may also be home to an enclave of females—though this is not always the case—who have little to do with each other. Each female tiger keeps to herself with or without her young. The male, being polygamous, will visit in turn the several females residing in his territory. Within each female's domain, peace reigns and contacts can evince a great deal of tenderness, both between partners and between the male and his offspring. The male usually has two or three female partners, occasionally four. Sometimes two females will band together to support each other, since everything depends upon their providing enough food for their young.

The largest tiger, the Siberian, has the widest territory. A male in search of prey, a task that has only

*Like all felines, the tiger marks his territory in different ways, notably by scratching the trunks of trees, much as a house cat scratches the legs of chairs and tables.*

grown more difficult, has a normal range of 1,200 to 1,600 square miles. The most extensive territory of a single Siberian tiger has been estimated to be almost 10,000 square miles. A female's normal territory ranges between 160 and 650 square miles. In certain areas of Nepal and India where prey is more abundant, tigers make do with much smaller areas: that of males can measure between 50 and 120 square miles, of females no more than 35 square miles. In general male Bengal tigers cover a range of 50 to 150 square miles, females 15 to 65 square miles—less than one tenth of the range of the Siberian tiger.

Above: *A Siberian tiger in captivity. Does it enjoy having nothing to do, or does it long for its vast lost territories?*

Following spread: *This magnificent Siberian tiger has just left an olfactory mark on the trunk of a fallen tree, as betrayed by his uplifted, curved tail.*

The extent of the territories of the other subspecies is not well known. Based upon total population, it is estimated that there are perhaps three Indochinese tigers for every 100 square miles and about the same for the Sumatran tiger. Insofar as the South China tiger is concerned, data from when they were plentiful does not exist and current research is hardly exhaustive,

since the animal has hardly been of interest to humans for reasons other than its extermination. This obviously did not encourage much scientific study. The same holds true for the three extinct subspecies.

## Killing to eat

On average a fully grown tiger needs about 20 pounds of meat each day, which makes it easy to see why they need such wide territories and large animals to prey upon. Whenever tigers are lucky enough to capture large animals, they stretch their supply of meat as far as possible. They can live on smaller prey when they have no other choice, but only for a limited time. After that they need to find larger prey. The Siberian tiger favors deer and wild boar, sometimes bear and eland, but it can also cast about for rabbit and won't pass up hare, badger, or lynx. The Bengal tiger is capable of tackling buffalo, small elephants, or young rhinoceros, but they prefer sika deer, gaur (large wild cattle of tropical Asia that are becoming rare), nilgai (an Indian antelope), and tapir, an animal that is most common in South America, but a species of which resides in Asia). If necessary the Bengal tiger will dine on monkeys, large rodents, or sea birds. Often the tiger attacks his prey in water while they are drinking. It also catches a variety of fish and crustacea in swamps, marshes, and rivers to augment its diet and has even been known to attack small crocodiles.

Power and endurance is often not enough to guarantee success in the wild; the tiger—which, one must

Above left: *A gaur* (Bos gaurus).

Below left: *A sambar deer* (Cervus unicolor).

Facing page: *Well-camouflaged in the underbrush, the tiger is on the lookout for its favorite prey, gaur or deer. In addition to poaching, the disappearance of these prey animals caused by their shrinking habitat accounts for the rapid decline of the tiger in the wild.*

not forget, is basically a cat—is endowed with extra-ordinary patience. Once it spots its prey, it can wait in hiding for hours until the right moment comes to seize its victim. Once its ambush is prepared, its striped coat and its ability to remain perfectly still renders it invisible even to those passing close by it. (This fact implies that it tolerates human presence to a much greater degree than the accounts of hunters might suggest.) Stalking in silence, it does not attack before it has gotten to within 30 or 40 feet, then leaps on the shoulders of its prey and goes for the throat. In the case of a large animal, the tiger will jump on its back and then tear at the nape of the neck. Often it will drop down on its prey from above. Its powerful jaws block the respiratory channels of its victim and shatter its spine for a quick kill. Bigger prey such as buffalo or large wild boar may well put up a fight. Its infrequent attacks on bear can lead to ferocious battles. The bear will not give up its life cheaply; sometimes

the tiger will lose its own or be forced to retreat from a power greater than its own. Since the tiger, like all other cats except for the lion, hunts alone, it only has its own strength and wisdom to fall back upon.

Whenever it is allowed to live in peace—which hardly ever happens—it is diurnal, although it likes to hunt at twilight or just before the break of dawn. Its excellent night vision gives it a definite advantage

Below: *A tiger staking its prey in high grass is practically invisible. By the time it makes its presence known, it is usually too late for its prey to escape.*

Right; *Tranquilly resting on a rocky promontory, this young tiger seems to be enjoying its continuing discovery of the world around it, as evidenced by its attentive and curious gaze.*

over most of its prey. But finding itself the target of human vindictiveness and hunted down even in nature preserves, it has long since become nocturnal.

As a general rule, large predators expend so much energy in the hunt that they rarely waste any of the nourishment they obtain. They tailor their behavior to the size of their prey. When a tiger kills a deer, buffalo, eland, or boar, it obviously cannot finish the whole animal at one time. But aside from the occasional fox or wolves (when there are any), few animals can benefit from the remnants of their repasts. The tiger will make the most of what it acquires. Like all cats, it will return to the carcass it has killed, dining upon it until only its bones remain. In the extreme eastern part of Siberia, the indigenous people refer to the tiger as the "Great Sovereign." They respect and venerate it as protector of medicinal plants, particularly ginseng. These people know that when the tiger kills a large animal, the other inhabitants of the forest can sleep peacefully for awhile.

It must be stressed that the tiger is not the bloodthirsty killer that the more far-fetched tales have portrayed. Nor is it the gentle pussycat so dear to advertisers peddling sugary cereals to children. Nor is it the jaunty and imbecilic yahoo that you put in your tank to speed your car along. That is a complete illusion: the tiger is not fast. Its top speed is no more than 35 miles per hour, for long distances no more than 15 or 20 miles per hour. Rather like the house cat, it is inclined to laziness. So what is it really? The tiger is sim-

*The top photo shows the tiger's preferred gait, a fast walk. It can only run flat out for short distances and rarely exceeds 30 miles per hour. (The lion's top speed can reach 50 miles per hour.) Like most large predators—whether mammals, reptiles, or fish—tigers know how to use their energy in the most economical fashion. This is essential for animals that hunt large prey.*

ply the most formidable predator in creation: nothing more or less.

## Family life

As with all good self-respecting cats, the tiger can be quite talkative. One can hear its roars from a mile or more away. Its vocalizing varies depending upon whether it is calling to a mate or to its children, declaring hostilities one male to another, or simply looking to make its presence known. It is one of three species of felines (along with the jaguar and one species of panther) that possesses a special cry that it emits when encountering one of its fellows on neutral ground: a sort of salutation that at the same time says, "Watch out." It is a nasal cry, a sort of "oof" that in German is called *prusten* (literally, to snort). Within its family circle, it mixes groans and roars, and in moments of extreme intimacy, when mating or between young tigers, one hears tender murmurings. Yes, it is true, the most ferocious beast of the jungles and forests of Asia, the uncontested master of his domain, can purr as gently as a tomcat lying by a fire, though its purring is not exactly the same. The domestic cat purrs while both exhaling and inhaling, so that it makes a continuous sound, but the tiger purrs only while exhaling. Nonetheless purr it does, expressing the close bonds

*Young love: two Siberian tigers.*

that exist within the members of its family and the pleasure it takes in being among them. It is true that this togetherness only lasts a short while between male and female, just for their mating period, then each retreats to his or her own place. But the male will then come to visit the female and his young from time to time, if only to assure himself that they are doing well.

In principle, couplings can take place at any time during the year, but in general the most favorable time is from late November to mid-April. Young are born between the beginning of March and the end of July after a gestation period of three months. We have to speak in the plural when referring to coupling, since the male tiger covers the tigress as many as fifty times in the course of three or four days, and in some cases as many as twenty times in a single day.

This lovemaking will, as a general rule, produce two or three babies, though there can be as many as six cubs in a litter. A tigress gives birth in the protection of her lair. Cubs are born with their fur and weigh on average three pounds at birth. They open their eyes after a week or two. They are completely weaned in six months, but the process begins when they are two months old and start eating meat. At this early age they do not leave their mother's side. She guards them, as all cats do, with a nonchalant air that disguises total watchfulness. If they are threatened by any danger, she will change places with them in an instant. If the threat to them is grave (for example, from a male other than their father), she will launch herself at the intruder, often sacrificing her own life for her cubs. If this occurs, the attacking male will immediately kill the cubs. But his preeminence will

*The tiger is not a sociable animal, except for brief periods of mating during which the couple shares their territory. Young brothers and sisters live together, but at the onset of adulthood and sexual maturity, they go their separate ways.*

will be of short duration if the tiger who owns the territory comes upon him. Then it is a fight to the death.

Tiger cubs begin to hunt small game at the age of six months but remain within hailing distance of their mother. By a year and a half, they begin to establish their own independence. The process is a gradual one that can last up to one year, then they go off on their own and set up territories for themselves.

Only a minority of tiger cubs survive to adulthood. About 34 percent die within their first year of life, and another 30 percent do not make it past their second year. Thus more than half of all tigers die before reaching sexual maturity, which occurs between the ages of 3 and 6 for males and 3 and 4 for females. In addition, females have a better survival rate than males, which explains the male tiger's

polygamy. An orphaned cub of less than six months old has no chance of survival unless it very quickly comes upon another female who is willing to adopt it. At six months or older, its chances for survival increase, but obviously depend upon the extent to which the cub has learned to hunt and defend itself. The average life span of a tiger is about 10 years, though they sometimes live to as old as 16.

It is thus easy to understand the precarious position of the tiger. Not only is it being senselessly hunted down, its own reproductive process adds to its difficulties. Its litters are small; it suffers from a very high rate of infant mortality; and it is unable to reproduce until a relati-

*The preliminaries are now over—preparing the female for intercourse is their primary aim—but that fact does not rule out displays of deep tenderness.*

vely late age. That said, left to its own devices in a relatively stable environment populated with a sufficient number of ungulates, it can manage quite well, as it did for millennia before the human species was able to check its development.

Above: *Exploring the world, the young tiger proceeds at a gallop.*

Right: *This tiger cub was afraid of the photographer.*

Following spread: *This still clumsy young tiger calls for its mother. What chance for survival does human folly allow it?*

# The Tiger and Man

To say that the relationship between tigers and humans has not been a beautiful love story is an understatement. At most, it is a love story that ends badly, since the tiger is today being driven from almost all of its habitat, even though this was not always the case.

As witness to this, we can evoke the Five Tigers that we mentioned in our preamble, that were the symbols of a protective force, or the white tiger that was endowed with royal virtue. The cat is opposed to the dragon in Chinese magic. If it is there seen as a passive principle, this is balanced in Chinese alchemy where it represents the active principle of energy and spirit.

The Goddess Shakti, who represents for Hindus the energy of nature, rides on the back of the tiger, which is killed by her consort, the god Shiva.

In Siberia, as we have previously noted, it is considered to be the guardian of medicinal plants, thus instrumental in healing. For this reason it is highly esteemed. Other Siberian peoples look upon them as men who take the form of tigers only for a time. These people see many similarities in the behavior and demeanor of men and tigers.

And although, with the exception of Siberia, the instances of tigers attacking humans are few and far between, they are universally feared, apart from the problems arising from the human population explosion throughout Asia. The tiger is feared since it is viewed as a man eater. And it is true that even though humans are not its preferred prey, its attacks have spread terror in fields and forest, mainly in the nineteenth and

Below left: *This painting by Eugène Delacroix portrays a tiger drinking from a dish held by the god Bacchus. He depicts the Caspian tiger, a subspecies that is now extinct.*

Below right and facing page: *Bengal tigers. It is estimated that the 10,000 tigers in captivity in the United States is double the total number of tigers in the wild. A number of private individuals own one or more tigers. But the tiger is not a domestic animal. Since 1990, captive tigers have killed 11 people and injured more than 60. Far better would be to let the tiger live in the wild and work to preserve its habitat and freedom.*

early twentieth centuries.

In point of fact, tigers kill people for various reasons, most stemming from the degradation of their living conditions, human encroachment, and environmental destruction, as well the lessening numbers of the tiger's normal prey, which are also being hunted. This state of affairs has led to more frequent encounters between the two species, and the tiger's realization that humans are fairly easy prey. At the same time the intense hunting to which it has been subjected in the last two centuries has taught the tiger to mistrust and avoid human contact wherever possible. In fact the only place where people are still being killed by tigers is in the mangrove forest of Sundarbans. Its inaccessibility has made hunting difficult. But this environment is being lost to increasing population pressures in Bangladesh, and the more frequent contacts with tigers often have fatal consequences for the inhabitants of the area. To prevent attacks, Bangladeshis wear masks behind their heads, showing a face, a subterfuge that often works to keep tigers at a distance. This practice is based upon the recognition that the tiger always allows its prey to pass it before attacking from behind. Seeing the cardboard face looking at it, it usually decides not to attack.

Sometimes sick or physically diminished tigers will attack humans since they are unable to take down their preferred prey; tigers who have lost or broken teeth are also dangerous since this prevents them from killing larger animals. Lastly, tigers may be surprised by humans who stumble upon them, and attack to defend themselves.

*Handicapped by the loss of its canine teeth, this tiger would no doubt attack humans, who are easy if not preferred prey. This condemns it to death unless it has the good fortune of living in a nature preserve or game park. By reproducing, it can help to prolong the life of the species.*

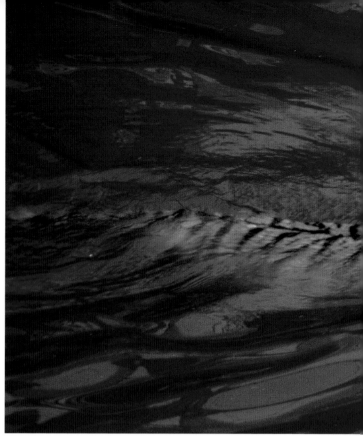

*This Siberian tiger lives in his natural environment in a preserve. For how long? The tiger's end is quickly approaching despite international measures to protect it. Its territories too often abut areas with burgeoning human populations. Interspecies encounters sometimes become conflicts in which the tiger is the inevitable loser. It is sad to reflect that the Five Tigers soon will be found only in captivity, wiped out by our heedlessness.*

With the construction of paved highways in northeast China, roads now cross through the territories of the Siberian tiger, and thousands of workers are often in close proximity to them. We do not seek to minimize the gravity of tigers' attacks on humans, but many more workers die because of inhumane working conditions than at the claws of the fearsome tiger. At

the beginning of the twentieth century when its environment was still relatively intact and its prey abundant, it had no reason to attack humans and did so only under extreme circumstances or when it itself was attacked.

Despite official measures to protect the tiger, which are now in force pretty much everywhere, it is a losing battle fighting against the traps and poisons laid by poachers, who do not observe national laws or boundaries. Poachers are many times more numerous than guards, who are responsible for overseeing vast territories. Sadly the price for a dead tiger is many times that of a live one. The problem is a global one. The effects of overpopulation are most sorely felt by the poorest countries, whose inhabitants experience such deprivation and misery that they will do anything to feed themselves and their families. It is hard to blame

them, even if one deplores and feels a justifiable anger about such deleterious consequences. It is not the poacher who is ultimately responsible; it is the illicit traffic in endangered species, which profits those least at risk and puts at risk those who are most vulnerable.

Thus the great animal spirits die out, causing in turn the disappearance of hundreds of other species, animal and vegetable, more humble and less visible. So the great forests and jungles are eradicated, and perhaps one day we will find ourselves alone faced with the wasteland we have created, with only our domestic animals as company. The "Great Sovereign" will have long since departed.